Alan Windsor Richards, 1960.

Einstein As I Knew Him

Alan Windsor Richards

HARVEST HOUSE PRESS
Princeton, New Jersey

Grateful acknowledgment is due
The Institute for Advanced Study,
Princeton, New Jersey;
The Princeton Packet; Princeton Alumni Weekly;
The Daily Princetonian; Trenton Times,
and the American Jewish Ledger for
their kind cooperation.

Library of Congress
Catalog Card Number 79-84421

ISBN 0-89523-001-1

Published in the United States
by Harvest House Press
Princeton, New Jersey

10 9 8 7 6 5 4 3 2 1

For Glenda

Contents

Editor's Preface

This book is not so much about Albert Einstein, the physicist, and his contributions to science, as it is about Albert Einstein in his later years—a resident of Princeton, New Jersey, and a member of that community.

As highlights of his thirty-year involvement with Princeton University in his role as official photographer, Alan Windsor Richards especially values those occasions when he was asked to photograph Dr. Einstein.

Some of the exchanges that occurred during these picture-taking sessions between the photographer and the scientist have become treasured memories of Alan Windsor Richards, and he has put them down here for us to enjoy.

I believe that you will find Mr. Richards' recounting of his experiences with Dr. Einstein to be not only engaging, but capable of illuminating our perceptions of those aspects that mark us—scientist and layman alike—as human.

Elisabeth Gerson

Princeton, New Jersey
1979

The notion of the "future" has meaning only in the realm of the 'between,' in the reciprocity between persons. In that persons have to do with one another and give themselves to one another, they are there for one another. It is only in this being with and for another that there can be any such thing as a future at all.

—Heinrich Ott
from *Gott,* 1971

Reflections

by Marvin Goldberger

I met Albert Einstein only once. In the spring of 1954 he attended a theoretical physics seminar at Palmer Physical Laboratory at Princeton University being given by H. P. Robertson from Caltech, a former Princeton professor. I was sitting alongside Eugene Wigner and Einstein was in front of us. After the seminar, Wigner introduced me. This sole contact scarcely qualifies me as an expert on Einstein the man, but every physicist is an expert on Einstein the scientist.

No single person since Newton has had so profound an influence on science as has Einstein. In the single year of 1905 he made three fundamental contributions to physics. In his paper on the electrodynamics of moving bodies he put forth his so-called special theory of relativity. The clarity of his presentation and his recognition of the necessity for the modification of the laws of mechanics to properly treat bodies moving at speeds comparable to the speed of light was, in itself, a remarkable achievement. It must be said, however, that this development was in the air at the time. Because of that and the existence of earlier work by Lorentz and Poincaré in the same area, in all probability someone would have come up with essentially similar views, perhaps a little later.

His second paper, on the photoelectric effect (for which he received the Nobel Prize in 1922) was really more dramatic. Einstein seized the idea, first vaguely introduced by Planck, that electromagnetic radiation in reality consists of "lumps," or quanta which we now call photons, and the energy of these photons is a constant (Planck's constant) times the frequency of the light. He showed how the energy of electrons emitted from the surface of a metal when it is illuminated could be simply and elegantly understood on this new quantum basis. These ideas of Planck's had been languishing since his explanation of black body radiation and it is not clear when they might have been picked up had it not been for Einstein's insight.

The third paper of the 1905 series was a quantitative theory of the erratic motion of small particles suspended in solutions called Brownian Motion. This development solidified the atomic theory of matter and provided a determination of a fundamental constant of nature, the number of atoms in a molecule of any substance. This work was a nice piece of mathematical physics based on Einstein's deep grasp of statistical mechanics but not as profound as the other two papers.

Although he made many extremely important contributions to physics before and after 1915, that year marks the crowning glory of Einstein's career: the creation, and there really is no other word for it, of the theory of gravitation. This is what is more popularly called by the misnomer 'the general theory of relativity' (to be contrasted with the 1905 "special" theory of relativity). The theory of gravitation fell like a thunderbolt on the scientific world. It came entirely out of the blue. I believe that had Einstein not lived it would have been fifty years at least before anyone would have taken this giant step. This theory, spectacularly confirmed by experiment, was a profound inspiration, the like of which we may never see again. It is a privilege to have lived through part of this era of discovery, especially now when the full implications of the theory of gravitation are playing an important role in modern astrophysics and cosmology.

February 19, 1979

What we must *learn is to order the human over the purely intellectual; purpose over power; the kind over the unkind; and the disciplined and spartan over the careless and self-indulgent.*

—E. Gerson
from *A Penny, A Pencil, and*
A Pound of Love:
Education Redefined, 1961

Reminiscences

by Alan Windsor Richards

In 1944, shortly before I came to Princeton as a photographer with the University, I was driving along Mercer Street at dusk, when half-way down the block, at street level, I saw a bodiless head—just two arms outstretched above it and a strangely familiar mop of shaggy white hair. Acting on professional instinct, I jumped out of the car, camera in hand, and snapped a picture. Only then did I hear the croaking sounds he was making and see the strained expression on his face. I rushed over, grabbed him under the arms, and hauled out one of the greatest scientists the world has ever known. Albert Einstein had fallen down an open storm sewer.

As I walked him the short distance to his home at 112 Mercer Street, he implored me in a flood of German-accented emotional phrases, mingled with sobs of pain, not to publish the picture. I promised him I wouldn't and I never did. Actually, I couldn't have even if I had wanted to. When I got home that night I discovered the picture was a blank. In my excitement I had forgotten to pull the film slide.

Off and on for the next twelve years of our association, Professor Einstein reminded me of my promise about the manhole picture. It got to be a kind of joke between us; but I could never bring myself to tell him that the last laugh was on me. I was ashamed—partly, I think, because of a math teacher who had made me feel a hopeless failure when I was a schoolboy back in Scotland. At my age, I didn't want to be tagged a dunce all over again, and I was still leery of mathematicians. In fact, I half expected Einstein to behave and dress the way my teacher did.

Shortly after our unorthodox introduction, I made the first of many appointments to photograph him officially. I arrived at his home on the dot and after persuading his secretary, Helen Dukas, that this was a valid assignment, approached his study. I was prepared to find him waiting impatiently in a wing collar and frock coat, with all the dignity of his genius. Instead, this world-famous figure was dressed in baggy slacks and an old sweater, his mustache scraggly, his hair looking as if it hadn't been cut or combed for months.

I was appalled. This was to be an official birthday portrait. I wondered why, since he hadn't done anything about the rest of his face, he had bothered to shave. I could hardly suggest that he spruce himself up for my camera, though on several occasions later I did try surreptitiously to brush his hair back behind his ears—accidentally, as it were, while arranging the lights behind his chair. But the unruly swatch always sprang forward again with a stubbornness of its own.

I gave up on his hair, but his feet continued to bother me. I am a Britisher by birth, with ideas perhaps too rigid about proper apparel. Professor Einstein seldom wore socks. Although I tried to take all his pictures from the knees or waist up, it was difficult to keep my eyes off those bare ankles. I even considered sending him an anonymous gift of a pair of socks, but that would have been not only insulting but useless.

Besides, during those first assignments I was constantly afraid that he would refuse to pose for me. I derived considerable prestige from the photographs I was privileged to take of him. Requests from all over the world were referred to me by the Institute for Advanced Study and by Princeton University. Two of my Einstein prints were reproduced on covers of *The New York Times Magazine*. I couldn't afford to antagonize so important a subject, and what worried me was that he just barely tolerated the business of having his picture taken.

Once when I brought him a dozen extra prints of a particularly good portrait to give to his friends, he flipped through them, then shoved the whole batch aside. "I hate my pictures," he said. "Look at my face. If it weren't for this," he added, clapping his hands over his mustache in mock despair, "I'd look like a woman."

On another occasion, when a young couple, at whose wedding he had been best man, brought their son—a little boy of 18 months—to meet him, the child took one look and burst into a screaming fit. The parents were speechless with embarrassment, but Einstein's eyes lighted up. He smiled approvingly, patted the youngster on the top of his head, and crooned: "You're the first person in years who has told me what you really think of me."

I was convinced that it would be extremely difficult to keep the cooperation of a man with so little vanity. At the same time I kept expecting him to change into my private notion of the way a world genius should be— proud, brilliantly erudite, perhaps somewhat impatient with men of lesser intellect.

But he didn't change. Instead, I think he changed me a

little. Gradually I lost my awe of him. So much so that one day I blurted: "Professor Einstein, why don't you wear socks?"

As soon as I'd said it I was dismayed at my own recklessness. But the remark didn't seem to faze him. "Oh," he shrugged, lifting his trousers a bit and glancing down, "it would be an awful situation if the containers were of better quality than the meat."

The way he said it—with humor, but sadly, too—made me realize that his sloppy sweat shirt and uncombed hair and sockless shoes were somehow right for him. They truly reflected the humility of the man. If I'd taken his picture any other way, I would not have got Einstein. I would have got my own image of how a great scientist ought to look.

Thus Einstein taught me something about photography: that I must approach a subject with an open mind as well as an open shutter.

Besides humility, I began to sense another quality behind Einstein's unkempt appearance: a profound simplicity that allowed him to ignore superficiality and go directly to the heart of things. Where most of us are like kites caught in the branches of trees, entangled with our concerns for such things as comfort, success, the impression we are making on others, Einstein's mind soared free. I doubt that he even knew what he ate. Certainly, he didn't watch where he walked, or he wouldn't have fallen down that storm sewer. Once when a company had sent him a very sizable consulting fee, he used the check for a bookmark and lost the book.

During the years that I knew Dr. Einstein, I collected many interesting anecdotes about his life: some were about events that occurred in Princeton while I was with him, others were told to me by different people. But I recall one very distinctly that happened right after the matter of Dr. J. Robert Oppenheimer, Director of the Institute for Advanced Study. Dr. Oppenheimer was in some sort of trouble with the Atomic Energy Commission concerning security. One afternoon, perhaps the day after Oppenheimer had been questioned at the Institute, I wasn't very far away from Einstein's house when I saw the old man being helplessly pushed around by a photographer and a man with a microphone rudely backing him off the sidewalk and firing questions at him. I didn't know what was going on, but I didn't think it was right and I remember going over to these fellows and telling them to let him alone. Einstein was saying that he had made a statement for Oppenheimer that morning at the Institute and that's all he would have to say. Actually Dr. Einstein had nothing whatever to do with the Oppenheimer problem, but they were trying to pump him for information.

I certainly was very much discouraged to see two men of the press taking advantage of him. I remember telling Einstein how mortified I was that any professional colleague of mine should behave in that way. I said, "We do pride ourselves—most of us—on being what is known as 'gentlemen of the press.'" I recall saying to him, "Dr. Einstein, those fellows must have really annoyed you terribly and made you very angry." "Oh no," he said, "I don't pay any attention to those things. You know anger dwells only in the bosoms of fools."

On another occasion I was in his study preparing to take some pictures when I found him feverishly jotting in a notebook, not even aware that there was a cut on his face. The two bright streams of blood were running down his cheek. I was so alarmed that I interrupted him to suggest that I go to the medicine cabinet and get a bandage. "Oh," he muttered, "it's not a matter of importance. It'll stop," and he went on writing.

I think one of the most amusing episodes took place in Princeton quite a number of years ago. A small girl had been given some homework by her teacher and she was quite unable to do it. On leaving school she was very much distressed because she realized that if she didn't succeed in her effort, she would probably receive a reprimand from the teacher the next morning. She decided then to talk to one of the other pupils and ask him if he could help her. He said, "No, I can't help you, but I'll tell you—on your way home up that street and about three or four houses to the right, in a yellow house, you'll find a man named Einstein who is very good at arithmetic. If you stop there, maybe he can help you." So the youngster decided that this was the course that she should follow and she started off up the road, finding her way to Einstein's house. This youngster didn't know that Einstein had a title such as Professor or Dr., so when she arrived at the house she rang the doorbell, and when the person in charge came to the door and asked the girl what she wanted, she said, "I'd like to see Mr. Einstein. There is something I would like him to help me with." "Well," the person at the door said, "I don't know if he is home." Just then Dr. Einstein came down the stairway and he saw the little girl standing in the doorway and asked her what she wanted. The little girl told him she had an arithmetic problem she couldn't do and it was her homework and she was terribly worried about it. She wanted to know if Mr. Einstein would help her. The Professor said, "Come on in and sit down with me on the couch and we'll talk about it."

When the youngster came in, Professor Einstein saw that the arithmetic problem was a simple one. He talked to her a bit and finally said, "You know, I don't think that I can do this: I don't think that I can. It would be very unfair to you and to your teacher if anybody else did this for you. You must learn in life to do things for yourself; and your teacher, whom I happen to know, is a good teacher who will help you. I think tomorrow morning when you go back to school, you'd better explain to her that you don't understand this and ask her to help you. I'm sure she will."

Of course the little girl was disappointed. She didn't know what to say, but Einstein continued, "No, it would be very unfair and it would be quite wrong if I did it. I can't do it. I couldn't do it." The little girl took the statement literally, and although she thanked him, she was disappointed. But she didn't tell her mother that night anything about what had happened.

She waited until the next morning in school; and then she went to the teacher and told her what had happened.

She said, "Miss Brown, I am sorry but I don't understand this problem you gave me to do. I had trouble with it." At this stage, the girl felt quite bold, because she had the moral backing of Einstein behind her. She said to the teacher, "Yesterday afternoon on my way home, I heard about a Mr. Einstein, who they say is quite good at arithmetic, and would be able to help me with my homework because I didn't understand it, and I didn't want to come here not doing it because I thought you would be angry."

"Surely," the teacher said, "you didn't go in and bother Dr. Einstein, did you? That was an awful thing to do." "Oh," the girl said, "it was no bother at all. He was very glad to see me. He was very kind to me and he took me into his living room and we sat on the couch and talked together. He told me that it was impossible for him to help me. It would be unfair to you and to me, and if he did it, it would be all wrong. But he did say that he knew who you were, that you are a good teacher, and that you would be able to help me. You see, Miss Brown, you *must* be a very good teacher if you can do this, because, you know something? I can't do it and also, poor Mr. Einstein—he couldn't do it either."

What struck me most was that Einstein automatically

ignored the trivial, whether it happened to be the cries of a child who was afraid of him, the rudeness of strangers, a cut on his cheek, or the pleadings of a little girl for help with her homework. He simplified his concerns in order to spend his time wisely. But it wasn't just a matter of withdrawing or of being "absent-minded." For this same uncluttered attitude allowed him to speak directly, with unaffected kindness and respect, to every human being he met, child or adult, ignoring externals.

On one occasion I was with Einstein in his study at his home, going over some pictures with him. Something occurred then that was one of the strangest things that had ever happened during the twelve years I knew him. I call it his elevation of a photographer's worth.

We had always been on a completely professional basis, and had never discussed anything much about our personal lives. This was something I never thought would happen. Now it seemed that suddenly this special genius had come down from the cosmos to the level of a layman like myself. I sat beside him on the couch and as we were looking at some pictures I saw in his face and in his voice a tremendous strength of character, a sincerity of purpose in all that he did. Perfection was his goal and obviously he had achieved it many, many times. Somehow he now seemed to think that it was important to convey to me some thoughts about the value of my profession. As he looked at my pictures he said, "You know, photography is a wonderful profession. You have done very well, but have you ever stopped to think that your profession and your activity with a camera is quite similar to the responsibility of a surgeon, who, with his scalpel, always has a life in his hands." Then he continued, "You have a life in your hands every time you use your camera and are photographing someone, because the picture you take today you may not get tomorrow, so you have to be very, very careful."

He went on to say, "Have you ever stopped to think that a photograph can be very kind?" "Well," I said, "Dr. Einstein, I don't — how do you mean, kind?" This was his answer: "A photograph never grows old. You and I change, people change all through the months and years, but a photograph always remains the same. How nice to look at a photograph of mother or father taken many years ago. You see them as you remember them. But as people live on, they change completely. That is why I think a photograph can be kind."

"You know," he continued, "whether you are taking a photograph of an old man, a lady, a little boy, or a dog—

that picture may well become the priceless treasure of a lifetime to someone later on."

That was certainly true, for all of the pictures that I have taken of him over the years are indeed priceless treasures of my photographic career.

The gentle touch of his genius quickened my own life as it must have that little girl's and the lives of so many others with whom he had even the slightest contact. It would be silly to claim that he and I ever became close friends. Names, like appearances, were unimportant to him. But he always knew who I was, and sometimes he would stroke my arm, delighted to see me. I think he liked and trusted me. It made me feel almost protective about him; yet so direct and compassionate was his perception that I felt that he understood more about me than I did myself.

One morning in his study at the Institute for Advanced Study, after a tiring picture session, I caught sight of his blackboard, covered with chalk hieroglyphics. I don't know why, but for the first time the mathematical equations seemed to mock me. I stood gazing at them blankly. Then the chalk marks went blurry and I shut my eyes. For that fraction of a second, I was being kept after class and my teacher was standing just behind me, glowering, knowing perfectly well I was stumped and ready to call me stupid.

I shook my head and turned around. Instead of my childhood mathematics teacher, there was Albert Einstein, quietly watching me. "Professor," I said, with an attempt at flippancy, "you and I are at opposite poles—you may be the world's best mathematician, and I may be the world's worst."

He shook his head and laughed softly. "Don't worry about that now," he said. "You have done well in your business. And you know," he added, looking at me with an expression full of intelligence and sadness, "it may have been the fault of the teacher. Sometimes they don't know how to handle a youngster. They get you scared. Some don't even want to teach—they hate to teach, but forget about it—don't stumble on that foolishness now."

What he said was not only intimate and kind, but so true that it was comforting. For a moment I was stunned by the thought that it might not have been my fault entirely, that I might not have been so stupid after all. Through the most direct kind of illumination, he had dispelled a dark cloud that had followed me for many years.

It was then, I think, that I first made the connection

between those equations on the blackboard and his several kinds of simplicity: the uncluttered quality of his vision, the directness of his perceptions, his disregard for appearances and material trivia. His theories, which have altered our ideas about the universe and led to our present age in physics, were the products of insight rather than complex computation. He arrived at them almost completely by himself. He was not part of a collective laboratory effort. He had no complicated equipment. He had only his mind, working with pencil and paper, chalk and blackboard, and humble patience, piercing through the surface incidentals to new underlying principles.

His accomplishments seem to have come from more than mere brilliance—from a combination of humility and imaginative daring. Perhaps the very act of making his discoveries about matter stirred him with both a sense of wonder at what the human brain could perceive, and a feeling of insignificance from realizing how small a part man plays in the vast logic of the universe. When I asked Dean Ernest Gordon of the Princeton University Chapel how he would explain Einstein's combination of great intellect with apparent simplicity, he said, "I think it was his sense of reverence."

There is no record to show that he observed any particular liturgy or recognized any particular dogma, yet I, too, had the feeling that he was a devout man. "The Lord is sophisticated, but not malicious" are words inscribed in German on the mantelpiece in one of the mathematical rooms in Princeton's Fine Hall. Those were the words of Albert Einstein. I think it was this sense of reverence that kept him so humble. He felt the stirring of the spirit that made him aware of his mortality and insignificance in the face of the eternal and the infinite.

One photograph that I took of Einstein appeared some time ago in the *Princeton Packet* with a caption saying "He Died Young." Einstein, of course, lived just past his seventy-sixth birthday; but he was young in heart and spirit. Especially, perhaps, because he had so much time for youth. The article went on to describe what "young" is.

"What is 'young' — and when is it?

"Young is an attitude, a spirit. A way of looking at things. Of responding to them.

"It is not an age. Not a hairstyle or a piece of clothing or a musical beat.

"Young can be a child examining his first marigold

with wonder and delight . . . or Verdi at eighty-one, composing his finest opera.

"Young can be a teen-ager careening on a surf-board . . . or Einstein, in his seventies, still working on his unified field theory, sailing his boat, and playing his beloved violin.

"Young is not a monopoly of youth. It survives, and flourishes, everywhere the vision has been kept fresh, the muscles of the mind firmly toned, the juices freely flowing.

"Let's not cater to youth, for its own sake, for its shibboleths and slogans and styles of the moment, nor scorn it for any of those reasons.

"Instead, let's respect 'young' wherever it may be found; whether the beard is soft and curly or stiff and gray. Spirit has no color—it is always translucent, with its own imaginative sheen.

"Youth should be listened to. But young should be followed. There is no generation gap between the young of any age."

A few months before his seventy-sixth birthday, I took my last photograph of him. I planned to take some more on his forthcoming birthday. But he said, "No, come back when I am eighty—then you can shoot all day long." I think he felt that he didn't have very far to go. He was not at all well. On April 18, 1955, one month after his seventy-sixth birthday, Dr. Albert Einstein died in the Princeton Hospital of an aneurism. A ruptured aorta, the main artery in the body, can, of course, mean sudden death. In this particular case, the doctor felt that there was a good possibility of extending his life by surgery. But Albert Einstein absolutely refused surgery—he would not be operated on.

There were three great scientists in our time whose names began with the letter "E" and ended with the letter "N." They were, of course, Thomas Alva Edison, Dr. Albert Einstein, and Dr. George Eastman, the famous founder and pioneer of the Eastman Kodak Company. Dr. Eastman was indeed the Dean of photography. The comparison that I make between Dr. Einstein and Dr. Eastman is brought about by the fact that in the late thirties, when George Eastman died in Rochester, he had left a note on the table by his bedside. In the morning when he was found and this note was read, there were but six words on it:

"My work is done—why wait?"

I can't help feeling that perhaps, as Dr. Einstein lay

dying in the Princeton Hospital and refusing surgery, very similar thoughts passed through his mind. He had had enough. He didn't want surgery.

I asked Dr. Dean, who was his doctor, why it was not possible, when they realized that the situation was critical, to operate. "No," he said, "as long as he had his faculties and his vital signs, and could talk and understand what was being said, there was nothing I could do. Nothing whatsoever. We simply had to abide by his decision."

His brain was removed by his wish and donated to science. I had the opportunity later of talking with the pathologist who removed the brain. It was interesting to note that the doctor told me that if his brain and two other persons' brains were laid side by side on a table, you couldn't tell any difference among them. There was absolutely no outward or visible sign of anything extraordinary about his brain. The power and the potential of his knowledge came from chromosomes—the invisible and undetectable power that is contained in the cells of the body.

His remains were cremated near Princeton. There were fewer people at his funeral than at his birth. He had really chosen to go alone, as he had in his thinking much of his life. The world of science and hundreds of laymen would have jammed the road to his place of rest had there been such a spot; but his last wish was granted. There is no cemetery, no urn, no shrine, no marker. There does not appear to be anything left to mark his passing.

On a warm spring day, several months after his death, I went down to an area of the Institute with my camera to take a few pictures of the building as it stood then. The path that Einstein walked along has now been covered over. It is a long distance through the trees toward the building.

While I was there, a student from the Princeton Theological Seminary came up to me. He saw me with the camera and asked me what pictures I was taking. I said, "Well, young man, I'll tell you what I'm doing. I'm taking pictures of that building you see ahead of you. It's the famous Institute for Advanced Study, where Dr. Albert Einstein did some of his work; a place that has housed many fine scientists from all over the world." Then I asked him, "Did you study at all about Dr. Einstein in school? What do you know about him?" "Oh," the student said, "of course I know of him. I haven't had time to study much about him, but I would like some day to learn more about his work."

Then I said, "You know, he was not only a wonderful man in his knowledge of science, but he was a fine gentleman and a great humanitarian who was kind to all he knew. But what has saddened me most is to be unable to know where there might be something left to remember him by, because his body was cremated, and the ashes—well, nobody knows what became of them. Perhaps we are walking on them. I rather feel that he wanted nothing left behind; no shrine, no marker, no statue."

"I have observed so many times," I told the student, "the wonderful statue of Admiral Nelson on top of the huge pinnacle in Trafalgar Square in London, one of England's greatest heroes. And the Duke of Wellington, astride a horse, perhaps looking toward his adversary, Napoleon Bonaparte. I have seen the statue of Edvard Grieg in Norway and the beautiful graveside of the composer Jan Sibelius in Finland, where a monument in the shape and size of a beautiful organ has been built. But Einstein—nothing at all. It doesn't seem right, does it?"

"If that is what he wanted," said the student, "I can understand it. But I think that there is a monument if you look far enough." "What do you mean?" I asked. "What sort of monument, and where?"

"A monument that will always mark his career. His work. His work must surely be his everlasting monument." I wanted to add, "Yes, and his faith in the order of a universe that we are just beginning to understand."

Images

by Alan Windsor Richards

In spite of his perception of the endless conflict between good and evil, and the dark and light in human beings, Einstein consistently pursued his personal and intellectual goals.

Albert Einstein's home at 112 Mercer Street in Princeton, New Jersey.

The well-known Institute for Advanced Study in Princeton, New Jersey.

The first picture Alan Windsor Richards took of Dr. Einstein in 1944.

About a year later this picture was taken of Dr. Einstein in his study, enjoying his pipe.

Taken in March of 1949 on the occasion of Dr. Einstein's 70th birthday.

On a windy day in the spring of 1950, a young man took this picture of
the photographer and the scientist together.

David Ben-Gurion and Dr. Einstein in the professor's garden, taken in 1951.

Dr. Einstein and Rabbi Irving Levy, Jewish Chaplain of the Hillel
Foundation at Princeton University in 1947.

Dr. Kurt Gödel, Dr. Julian S. Schwinger, and Dr. Einstein at the
Princeton Inn on the occasion of the first Einstein Award.

In May of 1954, in Einstein's garden, Z. Gezari assembled his hand-built telescope to the delight of the professor.

After the telescope was assembled, Einstein said to Alan Windsor Richards, "What a wonderful piece of work and to think I've never made anything with my hands."

Dr. John Von Neumann and Dr. J. Robert Oppenheimer with the world's first computer built in the United States at the Institute for Advanced Study in 1952. This computer is now at the Smithsonian Institution in Washington, D.C.

The Danish physicist Niels Bohr visited the Graduate College at
Princeton in the late 40s and was photographed with students by Alan
Windsor Richards.

Alan Windsor Richards showing the professor his then-brand-new strobe light. After hearing Mr. Richards's explanation, Dr. Einstein said, smiling approvingly, "You are now involved in the bombardment of particles."

The last picture Alan Windsor Richards took of Dr. Einstein several
months before his death in 1955.

The way Einstein's desk appeared at the Institute just after his death, his last equations still visible on the blackboard.

A man comes into the stream of time, goes out of it, and what he leaves behind is his labor and his love.

Taken when the noted Jewish philosopher, Martin Buber, came to lecture at Princeton, this portrait has been reprinted widely.

Yet this is not the last word about the significance of Buber's message, or even of his relation to Christianity—and Christianity in any case is a many-sided reality. The whole story cannot be easily summarised.

We may, however, reach a practical conclusion which is of immense importance for the strategy of reconciliation: the Jew cannot, and the Christian ought not to, proselytise: there is no simple either-or between Jew and Christian; both are part of the one salvation promised to all peoples.

—Ronald Gregor Smith,
from *Martin Buber*, 1967

Considerations

by Robert C. Cowen

"Why should I be interested in Einstein?," my unscientific dinner guest asked as the Einstein centenary year opened. Why, indeed? Does his work really touch the life of a latter-day housewife? And why is it that nearly a quarter-century after his death, and in a rather vague sort of way, he continues to symbolize humanity's unending quest for cosmic order?

Surely it isn't only because he altered some of the foundations of modern physics. You could say as much for the German physicists Max Planck and Werner Heisenberg. Or, for that matter, the Dane Niels Bohr, who helped to develop the theory of quantum mechanics that explains phenomena on the atomic scale.

Yet when you want to compliment someone's keen scientific knowledge, you don't call that person a "Planck," or a "Bohr." You call him— or her— an "Einstein."

Einstein's importance for us, it seems to me, lies as much in his character and attitudes as in his scientific accomplishments. The humility, compassion, and humor, of which the public has been casually aware for many years, have been captured in Alan Windsor Richards's recounting of his personal encounters with the professor while photographing him. In addition to these qualities that have long earned our admiration, Dr. Einstein became a kind of surrogate for the explorer in each of us.

Einstein was not a popularizer. He wrote and lectured little to a general audience. He worked with abstract mathematics and abstruse concepts. Nevertheless, he asked the kinds of questions that intrigue most people.

What is the essence of physical phenomena? What is time and what is space? "The most incomprehensible thing about the world is that it is comprehensible," he observed. You don't have to master tensor calculus to savor such thinking.

Although the "theory of relativity" was in the background, Einstein received the Nobel prize in 1922 for elucidating the photoelectric effect by which light makes electrical current flow in photocells, such as the electric "eyes" that open doors. Nevertheless, it is "relativity" that was his great contribution. First came the special theory in 1905 which deals with phenomena as measured by observers in uniform motion relative to one another and which neglects gravity. This was expanded into the general theory, first published in 1915, that allows for general relative motion of observers and includes gravity.

Although Einstein's ideas met with skepticism and generated controversy, they gradually revolutionized the outlook of physicists. Much of his work has been abundantly confirmed and is now part of the standard equipment of physicists and engineers as well.

Einstein asserted, as a basic principle, that all physical phenomena do, in fact, conform to relativity and designed his theory so that the laws of physics have universal expression. He took as a matter of experimental fact that the speed of light in vacuum is the same for all observers regardless of their own relative motions. Out of such a simple proposition, he built the special theory. Commenting on the boldness of Einstein's vision, A.P. French of the Massachusetts Institute of Technology has remarked: "It was typical of Einstein, and a sign of his greatness, that he drew conclusions of the most far-reaching kind from a bare minimum of data. Lesser men often attempt the same thing, of course, but differ from the Einsteins of this world in that their grand conclusions or generalizations are usually false."

The most important implication of special relativity, or to use Einstein's phrase—the equivalence of mass and energy—is dramatically demonstrated in the release of nuclear power when a small fraction of an atom's mass is converted into energy. This concept is most pointedly manifested in experiments with subatomic particles.

As developed by Einstein, and later by other scientists, "relativity theory" has driven home the conviction that space and time cannot be considered to be separate factors. Only the unity of time and space—the space-time continuum—appear to correspond to reality. It's not a strange concept when you consider that the light by which you see a star left its source years ago. So you must refer to the star you see today as being located at such and such a point in space at such and such a time.

However, some consequences of the relativity of time seem more startling. Consider the twin effect, which predicts that if one of twin brothers makes a trip in space at close to the speed of light, he will return younger than his twin. This predicted "time dilation" is confirmed by the extended lives physicists observe in fast-moving particles.

We know now that physical phenomena depend on

the paths material particles and radiation take through space and time. The effects of gravity appear as distortions of the geometry of space-time which influences those paths. Space, for example, may be curved and time "dilated," meaning our clocks run more slowly the stronger the gravitational effect. Satellites move in closed orbits around earth because earth's mass curves space in its vicinity.

The satellites, traveling along direct paths, thus move in curved (that is, circular or eliptical) orbits. This really is no more mysterious than the fact that the shortest distance between two points on the curved surface of the spherical earth lies along a great circle.

During the 1960s and 1970s astronomers and physicists worked on physical occurrences that can be understood only by applying principles Einstein developed. These phenomena include powerful energy sources; violent events in galaxy centers; indications of "black holes" (dead stars that have collapsed to a density where their gravity is too strong for even light to escape from them). Thus general relativity has again moved to the forefront of physics.

Einstein was a bold thinker. Yet he relied more on intuition than on data. He spent his later years working toward a single unifying theory that could embrace all physical events. He never could accept the indeterminacy of quantum theory which holds that the physical state of a particle cannot be predicted exactly. Only the probability of its being in a given state can be foretold. Hence his famous remark, "God does not play at dice."

Perhaps Einstein's intuitive perceptions and hopes may yet prove to be correct. Astrophysics, particle physics, and cosmology are vital areas of contemporary scientific concern.

In 1975, the British physicist P.A.M. Dirac wrote, "I think that it is quite likely that at some future time we may get an improved quantum mechanics in which there will be a return to determinism and which will, therefore, justify Einstein's point of view. But such a return to determinism could only be made at the expense of giving up some other basic idea, which we now assume without question."

Thus it is that Einstein's work still challenges us to answer his question: "Is the world really the way it seems to us?"

About Marvin Goldberger

President
The California Institute of Technology

Dr. Goldberger was born in Chicago, Illinois in 1922. He received his B.S. in physics at Carnegie Institute of Technology (now Carnegie Mellon University) in 1943 and his Ph.D. at the University of Chicago in 1948. He was married in 1945 and has two children.

He served in the U.S. Army from 1943 to 1946, mostly in the theoretical physics division of the Metallurgical Laboratory at Chicago (a part of the Manhattan Project) working on neutron diffraction and on nuclear reactor design.

After a year at the Radiation Laboratory at Berkeley and a year as a research associate at the Massachusetts Institute of Technology, he went to the University of Chicago as assistant professor of physics in 1950. He became associate professor in 1952 and a full professor in 1955.

He was Higgins visiting associate professor at Princeton in 1953-54 and in 1957 joined the faculty at Princeton as Higgins Professor of Mathematical Physics, a position he held until 1977 when he became Joseph Henry Professor of Physics. He was chairman of the physics department at Princeton from 1970-76. Dr. Goldberger became President of the California Institute of Technology on July 1, 1978.

About Robert C. Cowen

Natural Science Editor
The Christian Science Monitor

Robert C. Cowen was born in Concord, New Hampshire in 1927. He received his S.B. from the Massachusetts Institute of Technology in 1949, and S.M. in 1950. He was married in 1955.

For over twenty-five years he has been a natural science specialist for *The Christian Science Monitor* and natural science editor. He believes that people want to understand the sciences—not fear nature's forces. His writing helps to dispel misunderstandings of science and replaces fear with information.

His 1977 series on facing natural disasters explains such earth forces as storms and earthquakes. The series illustrates how we can anticipate and take precautions to prevent major catastrophes.

Mr. Cowen has received a number of awards for his scientific writing, including the Grady Award—American Chemical Society; the Aviation and Space Writers Award; and for the series, *Coping With Nature's Forces,* the AAA–S—Westinghouse Science Writing Award—American Association for the Advancement of Science.

About the Author

Alan Windsor Richards began his association with Princeton University in 1944 when he became the Director of Photography at the Palmer Physical Laboratory. At that time the well-known Manhattan Project was underway.

At the close of World War II, Mr. Richards continued his photographic work for Princeton for over twenty-five years as photographer for the Public Relations Department of the university. He covered the Olympic games in 1948 in England and in 1956 in Melbourne, Australia for the U.S. Olympic Committee.

Born in Scotland on November 17, 1899, just ten miles from the home of Robert Burns, he was educated in Scottish schools and attended college in Edinburgh. He served in the British Royal Air Force in World War I. Mr. Richards spent several years, after coming to the United States in 1921, as photographer working with pathologists and medical technicians. His association with Princeton followed that period.

Mr. Richards is a Master Mason in the Blue Lodge of the Scottish Rite; a member of the Princeton Lodge No. 38, F & A M, and an honorary member of the Lodge of Rectitude in Sydney, Australia. He lives with his wife, Glenda, in Princeton, New Jersey.

Postscript

We are all here to learn from one another. Teachers, however, have a special kind of responsibility.

Some years ago, a student complained to Dr. Einstein about his teacher. The professor responded by placing his hands gently on the student's shoulders and saying,

> 'You should try to remember that a *dedicated* teacher is a valuable messenger from the past, and can be an escort to your future."

A statement surely worthy of our reflection.

Colophon

Title, conception and design	E. Gerson
Preparation by	Louis F. Conant III
Copy Editor	Mathilde E. Finch
Typesetting	Thomas McBeth, Image Graphics
Display type	Elizabeth Typesetting Co. Kenilworth, N.J.
Papers by	Kromekote, Meade and Varnoset
Printed by	Parker Printing Co. Trenton, N.J.
Bound by	Delaware Valley Bindery Trenton, N.J.
Available from	HARVEST HOUSE PRESS P.O. Box 978 Edison, N.J. 08817 201/225-1900
Sales Representatives	Publishers National Marketing Group Richard R. Ryen Oradell, N.J. 07649 201/261-7450